Working High and Low

Diana Noonan

Contents

Off to Work! 2
Jobs Up High 4
Jobs Down Low 18
Exciting Jobs 30
Glossary 31
Index 32

Off to Work!

Work is part of everyday life for many adults. People can work full-time, part-time, casually or in shifts. Some people work in unusual places, such as high in the sky or far beneath the surface of Earth. For these people, work is a different experience. They have to constantly think about safety when they are up in the air or underground, and it is difficult to take breaks if they are high in a tree or deep underwater.

Jobs Up High

High-Rise Window Cleaners

The world's tallest building is the Burj Khalifa in Dubai, United Arab Emirates. It is an incredible 829.8 metres tall. It takes 36 window cleaners three months to wash all of the building's 24 830 windows. The window cleaners wear protective clothing that looks similar to a **moonsuit**. Sometimes, they work in dust storms and high winds. They move around the outside of the building throughout the day, so they are never in direct sunlight.

It is important for the window cleaners of the Burj Khalifa to be protected from the sun, because Dubai is a desert city.

High-rise window cleaners need to carry the water or hose for washing the windows with them.

High-rise window cleaning is a skilled job. Cleaners either work solo, on **Bosun's chairs**, or in teams on platforms that hang from the side of the building. They are experts at tying knots and **rappelling**, and working with ropes and safety harnesses. In fact, high-rise window cleaning has been described as being more like rock climbing than washing windows!

High-rise window cleaners have to plan their day carefully. Each time they start their job, they must bring everything they will need with them, from pressure sprayers to soap and squeegees. There is no opportunity to go back for something they have left behind once they are 70 storeys up! For the same reason, bathroom and lunch breaks are scheduled ahead of time.

But even with careful planning, things can go wrong. High in the air, bugs or birds can attack without warning. Dangerous gusts of wind can make platforms tilt or sway, and bad weather can prevent people working for a period of time. Scaffolding can break and ropes can wear thin, and there are no safety nets when problems arise.

But despite everything that can go wrong, high-rise window cleaners say they would not change their job for anything. Every day, they are able to work outdoors. No one bothers them when they are so high off the ground, and they have the best views in the world!

Some high-rise window cleaners work in groups on shared platforms.

Arborists

Arborists use their skills to give diseased or damaged trees the best chance of a long, healthy life. At the same time, they try to keep people who live or spend time near trees safe. As arborists go about their work, they are many metres off the ground, wearing a harness that is attached to the tree by a rope.

Arborists have to be very skilled at tying and untying knots.

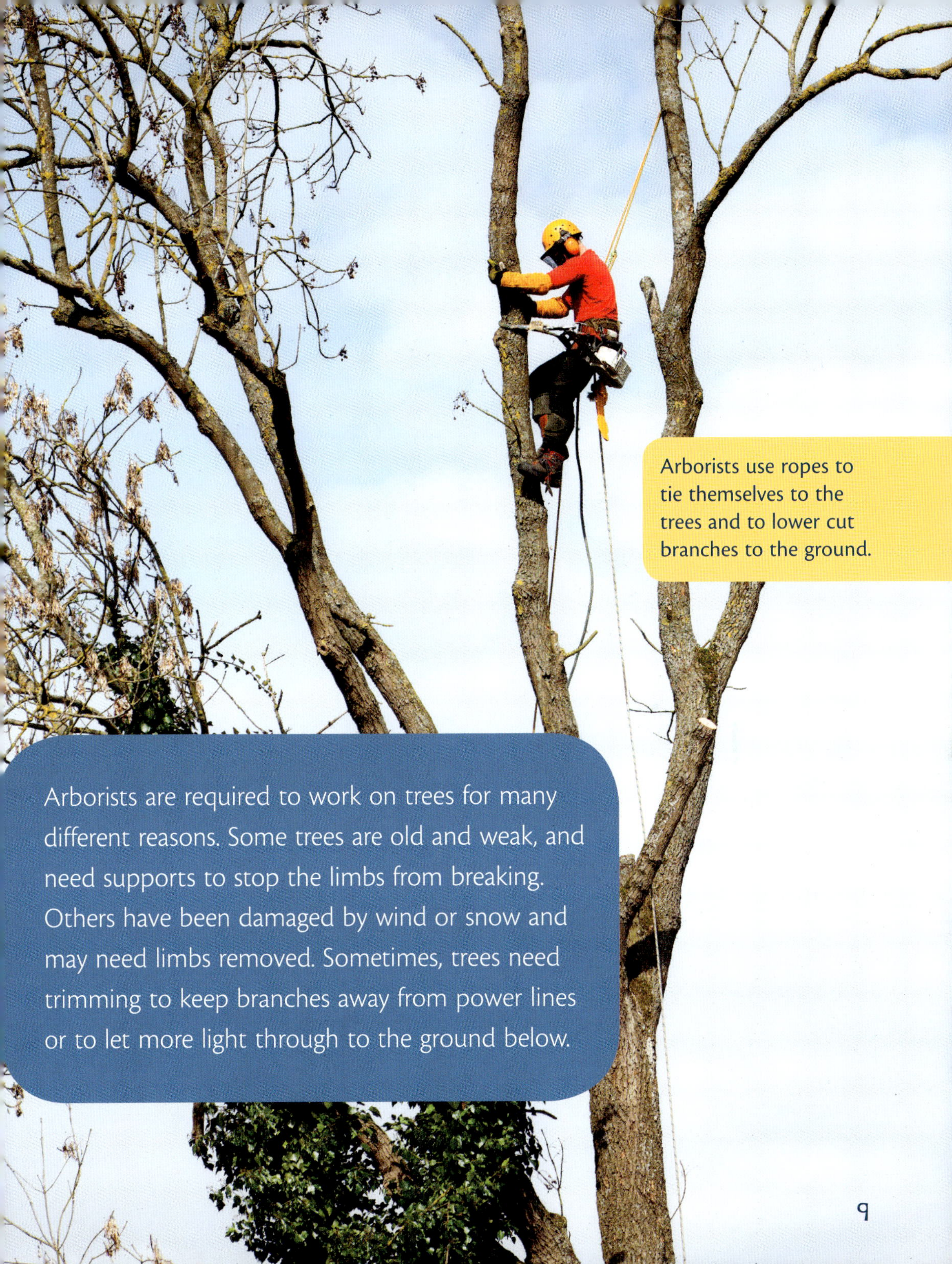

Arborists use ropes to tie themselves to the trees and to lower cut branches to the ground.

Arborists are required to work on trees for many different reasons. Some trees are old and weak, and need supports to stop the limbs from breaking. Others have been damaged by wind or snow and may need limbs removed. Sometimes, trees need trimming to keep branches away from power lines or to let more light through to the ground below.

Arborists use ropes rather than heavy equipment to complete their work. Big equipment can compact the soil around the base of a tree and stop much-needed oxygen reaching its roots. Arborists are also skilled climbers, who know how to attach themselves securely to a tree. They wear a special harness with loops to hold equipment, such as different kinds of saws, tools and climbing gear. It takes a lot of strength to climb into a tree and remain steady as the work is completed. Arborists have to stay fit and healthy to do their job.

Arborists use manual saws as well as power tools to cut branches from trees.

Arborists are specially trained to know just how and where to cut branches, and how to lower trimmings safely to the ground. Their training also helps them to stay safe around electric cords and fast-moving power tools. But no matter how careful an arborist is, and how much they enjoy caring for trees, their job is never easy, and is always dangerous.

Larger branches have to be lowered very carefully so they don't fall on whatever is below the tree.

Think and Talk About ...

Arborists are sometimes called "tree surgeons".

Flight Attendants

Flight attendants on domestic and international passenger planes work at **altitudes** of up to 12 000 metres. They help look after hundreds of passengers on flights that can last as long as 14 hours.

An emergency is difficult in any situation, but especially in the air. Passenger safety is an important part of flight attendants' work, before take-off and during the flight. Before the plane takes off, flight attendants make sure that the doors are closed securely, that passengers stay seated when asked to and that aisles are kept clear of belongings. They also show passengers what to do in case of an emergency.

Flight attendants begin every flight with a safety demonstration for the passengers.

Flight attendants make sure that all the passengers have enough to eat and drink during the flight.

Once in the air, flight attendants help prepare and serve drinks and meals in a very small **galley**. They **co-operate** with each other so that nothing gets spilled or dropped. When flight attendants are working in such cramped spaces, they try very hard to be helpful and polite to each other. During the flight, the plane has to be kept clean and tidy. Flight attendants clean the bathrooms and clear away rubbish.

It is important to keep healthy when on long flights. Flight attendants make time to eat their own meals and take breaks whenever they are scheduled. There are special crew cabins on board large planes where attendants can wash. These cabins also have small beds where attendants can rest during their breaks.

One of the problems flight attendants have to cope with is jet lag. Jet lag is the tiredness that comes from flying around the world from one time zone to another. To help fight jet lag, flight attendants drink plenty of water and eat fresh food. Although the plane may land in an exciting city, flight attendants always try to get to sleep as soon as possible!

On long flights, flight attendants take longer breaks in special cabins so they are able to sleep.

Space Station Astronauts

The International Space Station (ISS) travels at up to 27 600 kilometres per hour, about 400 kilometres above Earth. Six people work full-time on the ISS, conducting experiments and keeping the space station running smoothly.

The ISS has been orbiting Earth since 1998.

Think and Talk About ...

Astronauts live on the International Space Station for several months at a time.

The astronauts on the ISS live and work in a **micro-gravity** environment. This means they float around, and so does anything else that is not anchored securely. Food is in sealable pouches, so it does not drift away inside the space station. Both hot and cold drinks are drunk through a straw from sealed packets. Showering is impossible, so astronauts wash themselves with a wet towel. When the astronauts use their toilet, special pipes suck away the waste to storage containers. Astronauts stay warm at night in sleeping bags. Special fastenings secure the bag to the wall so the astronauts don't float around and bump into things while they are sleeping.

The astronauts on the ISS have to be strapped to the walls while they sleep.

In a micro-gravity environment, moving about takes almost no physical effort. Because of this, astronauts aboard the ISS exercise for two hours a day to keep healthy. They also look after their health by taking breaks, enjoying hobbies, talking to and messaging family and friends, reading and getting plenty of rest. One of the things astronauts enjoy during their spare time is looking out the window at planet Earth, far below, and watching the Sun rise every 92 minutes!

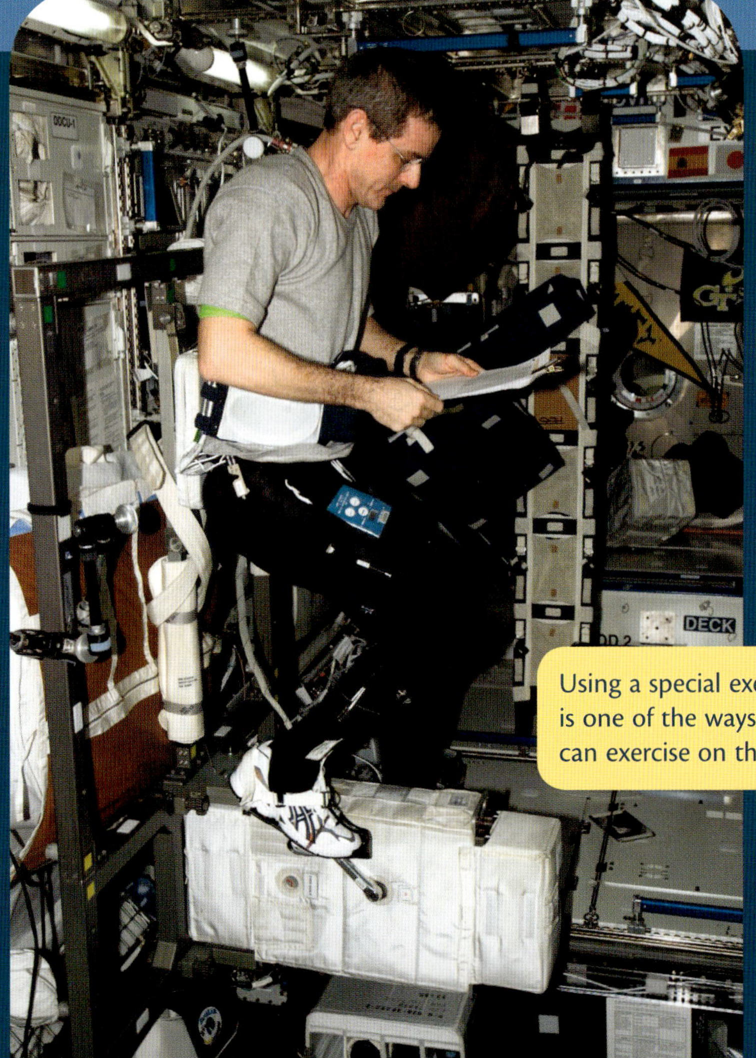

Using a special exercise bike is one of the ways astronauts can exercise on the ISS.

Jobs Down Low

Underground Train Drivers

Each day, far underground, trains carry millions of passengers to their destinations. It is the job of underground train drivers to make sure every passenger travels safely and arrives on time.

Underground train drivers sit at the front of the train in their own compartment. It is warm and comfortable inside, but it can be more bumpy and noisy than riding in a carriage of the train.

The Eurostar is a train that travels through a long tunnel under the English Channel.

Some people think underground train drivers must get bored and lonely, with no one to talk to and nothing to look at except darkness. But underground train drivers are kept very busy. They are always on the lookout for signal lights, the lights of a train in front of them, underground track workers and anything on the track. They have announcements to make whenever the train is stopping or starting, or if it is delayed or running late.

At stations, train drivers look back along the platform to make sure all passengers are safely aboard before the train starts moving. If a passenger pulls an emergency stop lever, the driver must check through each carriage to find out who pulled it and why. At the end of the day, the driver checks all the carriages for any passengers who may have fallen asleep and are still on board.

Underground train drivers don't just operate the train, they also have to be aware of any problems on the platforms or tracks.

It is not as easy to summon help underground as it is above ground, so drivers are well trained and know what to do in emergencies. They know how to **investigate** electrical or mechanical breakdowns, and how to respond to an emergency, such as a fire or an explosion. As they travel underground at speeds of up to 90 kilometres per hour, drivers have to pay attention to make sure every train arrives safely and on time.

The total length of the London underground train network is 402 kilometres.

Think and Talk About ...

The deepest underground train station is in Russia, and is 105 metres below the ground.

Cave Guides

Cave guides work in an environment that is very different from the world we live in every day. As well as being in darkness, caves can be full of **fragile** limestone formations, such as **stalagmites** and **stalactites**. These formations can be easily damaged if they are touched. Cave guides encourage visitors to stay on the walking track through the cave. They help to protect the underground environment for everyone to enjoy.

Caves are also home to fascinating but shy animals, including glow-worms, spiders, fish and bats. Cave guides make sure everyone speaks quietly and enjoys looking at the animals without touching them.

Caves are usually very dark, so cave guides make sure nobody gets lost in the darkness.

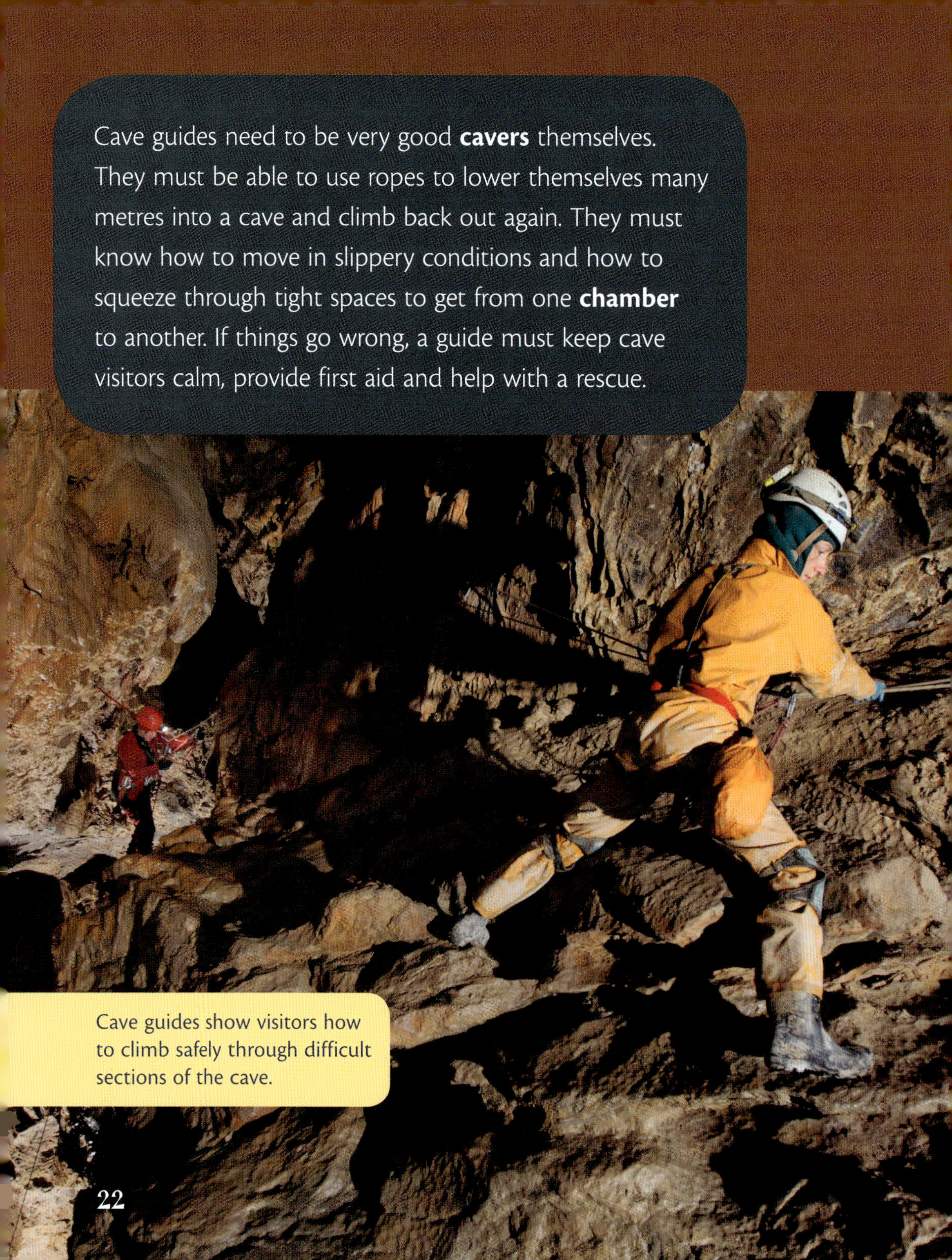

Cave guides need to be very good **cavers** themselves. They must be able to use ropes to lower themselves many metres into a cave and climb back out again. They must know how to move in slippery conditions and how to squeeze through tight spaces to get from one **chamber** to another. If things go wrong, a guide must keep cave visitors calm, provide first aid and help with a rescue.

Cave guides show visitors how to climb safely through difficult sections of the cave.

To keep everyone safe underground, cave guides check that visitors have the right equipment and clothing before they enter the cave. Warm clothes, strong shoes and a helmet with a headlamp are important. If visitors are exploring a cave by boat, they also need to wear a life jacket.

Cave guides work many metres below the ground to share with others a world they enjoy themselves.

If a cave guide is leading a tour by boat, they will need a boat licence.

Deep Sea Divers

All deep sea divers go underwater using special equipment to help them breathe. The equipment they use depends on how deep they go, how long they stay underwater and how many days they dive in succession. With the correct equipment and training, professional deep sea divers can go as far as 100 metres below the surface of the ocean.

deep sea diving equipment

Deep sea divers do different kinds of work. Some lay and mend underwater pipes and cables. Others help **salvage** wrecked ships. Some deep sea divers work with scientists to make new discoveries. The most common job for divers is to work for offshore gas and oil companies, or as scientific photographers.

Deep sea divers have a wide range of knowledge and skills. Many have studied science or **engineering**. Some are welders or bolt cutters, or are trained to handle explosives. It is important for deep sea divers to stay fit, as they may often be lifting heavy loads and carrying tools as they go about their work.

Underwater photographers need to carry a light source to light their photographs deep underwater.

Think and Talk About ...

Deep sea divers can work underwater for a maximum of about two hours at a time.

While they are underwater, deep sea divers see all kinds of sea life, from dolphins and killer whales to sharks and barracuda. Some sea animals can cause problems. Divers have been killed when manta rays have become tangled in their equipment and pulled the diver too quickly to the surface. But in spite of underwater dangers, many deep sea divers say that diving is like exploring outer space while still on Earth. They see parts of the world that few people have ever been to.

Deep sea divers are able to swim among sea life as part of their daily work.

Think and Talk About ...

Astronauts often train deep underwater before they travel into space.

Underground Coal Miners

Underground mining is sometimes called "deep mining". Underground coal miners work as deep as 300 metres below the surface of Earth. No sunlight reaches the bottom of the mines, so miners use **cap lamps** to help them see.

Miners travel to their mining site in a mantrip. A mantrip may be a truck, which drives along a specially built underground road, or it may be a vehicle, similar to a small train, which runs on rails. Some miners travel straight down in a lift to meet their underground mantrip.

Underground mines can be vast networks of tunnels, so miners ride in mantrips to move about the mine.

Once they are underground, miners have different jobs to do. Some drive trucks that carry coal to conveyer belts or to the surface. Others operate the heavy machines that **gouge** out the coal from the walls of the mine. Some miners are skilled at using explosives, which are sometimes used to break open rock in the mine.

Some underground coal miners use large drills to form new tunnels.

Think and Talk About ...

Underground mining is used to find precious metals and gemstones, as well as coal.

Underground miners take great care when they work. They check for **toxic** gases, especially methane, which could cause an unexpected explosion or fire. They are always watching for signs of a **cave-in**, which could block their exit from the mine. They take care not to become caught in the moving parts of the heavy machinery they work with.

To help them keep safe underground, miners wear protective clothing, such as gloves, earplugs, steel-capped boots and safety glasses. They carry special equipment, including a gas detector and **self-rescuer**. Most importantly, miners become close friends with the people they work with, and everyone looks after one another.

Miners sometimes have to repair the machines they use underground.

Exciting Jobs

While many people earn their living working in an office, other people work in unusual locations. Some people have jobs far above the ground, such as cleaning the outside of skyscrapers, working high in trees, flying on aeroplanes and even managing the International Space Station! Other people work beneath the surface of Earth: driving underground trains, guiding visitors through caves, diving deep underwater and mining for coal. The people who work in these high and low places consider themselves very lucky to have such interesting jobs.

Glossary

altitudes (*noun*) heights above ground

Bosun's chairs (*noun*) devices to hold people above the ground while they work

cap lamps (*noun*) head lamps that fit over miners' helmets

cave-in (*noun*) the collapse of a mineshaft

cavers (*noun*) people who are skilled at finding their way through underground caves

chamber (*noun*) a room (or open space) in a cave

co-operate (*verb*) to work together

engineering (*noun*) the study of designing structures and machines

fragile (*adjective*) delicate or breakable

galley (*noun*) a small kitchen

gouge (*verb*) dig or cut

investigate (*verb*) check or find out

micro-gravity (*noun*) almost (but not totally) without gravity

moonsuit (*noun*) a sealed, protective suit

rappelling (*verb*) descending a wall on a rope, in a special harness

salvage (*verb*) recover or get back

self-rescuer (*noun*) a breathing system

stalactites (*noun*) a rocky formation growing from the roof of a cave

stalagmites (*noun*) a rocky formation growing from the floor of a cave

toxic (*adjective*) poisonous

Index

arborists 8–11
astronauts 15–17
Burj Khalifa 4
cap lamps 27, 31
cave guides 21–23
dangerous 6, 11
deep sea divers 24–26
Earth 2, 15, 17, 26, 27, 30
emergency 12, 19, 20
environment 16, 17, 21
equipment 10, 23, 24, 26, 29
explosives 25, 28
fit 10, 25
flight attendants 12–14
harness 5, 8, 10, 31
International Space Station (ISS) 15–17, 30
mantrip 27
micro-gravity 16, 17, 31
miner 27–29, 31
passengers 12, 13, 18, 19
platforms 5, 6, 7, 19
safely 11, 18, 19, 20
skilled 5, 8, 10, 28
squeegees 6
sunlight 4, 27
tools 10, 11, 25
train drivers 18–20
underground 2, 18–20, 21–23, 27–29, 30, 31
underwater 2, 24–26, 30
window cleaners 4–7